NEW DEMOCRACY

M. PERUMAL

Notion Press

Old No. 38, New No. 6
McNichols Road, Chetpet
Chennai - 600 031

First Published by Notion Press 2019
Copyright © M. Perumal 2019
All Rights Reserved.

ISBN 978-1-64587-688-5

DEDICATION

I dedicate these valuable thoughts to my parents, who's purest blood is the real inspiration for this creation. Without their existence I may not be here and without my existence this may not be here. It is a beautiful and purest breeze of democracy emerged from my mind which will cure major flaws in democracy and solve all kinds of problems in country and world. It is nothing but an evolution in democracy which will remove major corruption, maladministration, regional conflict, and religious fighting and give way to the most capable and most deserved people ruling the country and the world.

—M. Perumal

CONTENTS

1

OLDEN INDIA

Great Emperors and Kings were ruled the beautiful India, which had glittering gold's, sparkling diamonds, colorful emeralds, glorious pearls, precious metals and gems. Beautiful Queens, astonishing women's adorned the India. Wonderful Temples, unbelievable architectures, attractive paintings, charming statues, culture of different natures inspired the heart of everyone. Perennial rivers, ever green forest, uncorncorable beasts enriched the ancient India and attracted the people from all over the world. First ancient India and Indians conquered the heart of the others so that others conquered the India later. Bravery was in the blood of each and every ruler, Kings and Emperors. Mighty worriers astonished the kings and emperors in the wars and protected their kingdoms. But ambitions flowed in their hearts of all kings, emperors and warriors; art and beauty of nature and beauty of women attracted each one of them; wealth and desire influenced in their life. So there were no unity and co-operation among the Kings and

Emperors. Always one wants to be supreme on others. Wars and fights were common among them and were going on everywhere.

Much eager to acquire territory and wealth, they were ruthless in suppressing their enemies. Women and wine were the way of life. Emperors, kings and close people to kings, Jamindars and rich tasted the honey of life and eternal joys. Poverty was common for the most of the peoples; slavery suppression and torture by the mighty people were under unquestionable practice. Freedom of speech and liberty to live as they like for common

People were in their remote sense of life. Castes, creeds and religions were in strong hold, higher castes exploited the lower castes. Lower castes as well as poor people were working only for their food, beyond that they can't expect anything more.

Frequent draughts, famine and disease added fuel to the people's suffering and moved here and there for their lively wood. Castes, communities, religions, regions, wealth and poverty divided the people. Poor people have to work hard and harder for the rich and mighty people as bounded labor. Indian rulers had plenty of wealth and property. This has attracted foreigners to invade India. Exploiting the non-unity of the Indian Kings and Emperors, existence of castes, poverty and non-unity among the masses, foreigners had intention to invade India.

So Mogul invaded India, established their kingdoms and ruled till British domination. During their rule there were destructions of the Hindu Temples and culture; forced religious conversation from Hindu to Islam. There were always tension among Muslims, Hindus and other religions. As a trader British people came to India to acquire wealth. But they have seen the weakness of the Indian Rulers and People's separation by the way of castes and creeds. They had advantage on the act of suppression of the people and the submissive way of life. They observed that a small amount of the people only ruling the entire country and all others are slaves.

If they invaded the small amount of the people then the entire India will become under their rule. Ancient day only one man will have control on entire village and one Jamindar will have control on four or five villages. One small king will have control on so many Jamindars, so if a small king is captured hundreds of village will fall under them. With their force again they can attack another king. This technique the British people followed and they started capturing small, small place under East India Company. Majority of soldiers' in their army were Indians.

At that time other Indian kings who were ruling not resisted the British East India Company invasion. If they resisted in the beginning itself British could not established their rule in India. Indian rulers are very selfish; they get satisfaction by seeing the fall of other kingdom.

They never thought that they will also be the victim for one day and face the same situation. Later wards many kings fought individually for the freedom but what is the use only lost their kingdom, life and property.

After a long time of struggles and movements; after losing so many lives, kingdoms and properties, India got freedom.

2

INDIA AFTER FREEDOM

Now it is one of the biggest democratic countries in the world. Democracy becomes common in most part of the world, even though communism, dictatorship as well as king's rules exist in the others parts of the world. India is a democratic country.

For the past 70 years the country is ruled by democratic way of the elected representatives. In the meantime so many national parties emerged, some national parties died. So many regional parties emerged, some regional parties got divided.

No national party is getting two third majorities so the coalition government is forming. But we have to think now that is this kind of democracy without any flow? If there is a flaw what is the way and how to rectify this?

The present democracy may be well suited for the earlier days, so people were in favor of that, agreed and followed.

That was the first stage of democracy and no time left to the people and politician to evaluate the merits and demerits.

People were illiterate, no media like TV and Radio for the common people to know what is happening in their surroundings, in the other part of their own country and in the world. People could not read and able to understand fully.

So that all the time common people needed somebody to give information and educate them. So that new and new leaders rose in deferent part of the country to give information and news about what is happening other part of the country; what is politics? What is democracy? What is mean by freedom? And what are the living standards. What is their basic requirement for comfort living? So the leader needs a party and followers to communicate all to the public. With the result parties had selected the good orators as their candidates and stood in elections.

There were frequent Party meetings, party leaders and followers were addressing the gatherings hours together. People were flooding to here the speeches of the leaders. There were revolutionary speeches on suppression, ignorance and education. People overwhelmed by the speeches and started thinking about life and politics. They started supporting the parties and voted to their favorable parties and those who win with two third majorities is allowed to form a government to rule.

Now the situation has been changed completely. People have no time to listen the speeches. All the time they listen

Televisions, Radios and read news-papers, magazines and gathers more information than the speeches.

People came to know very well that speeches will be one sided and in favor of the one side only. People's analytical power and criticisms on any subject increased.

Awareness on politics and social economical life is increased. So at this juncture there is a need to think it over that is the present way of party system needed to rule the country? Is it suitable now? If not what is the alternate way for it?

3

INDIAN – DEMOCRACY

In Indian Democracy the lazy and sleeping people are more than awakening people. Parties are taking more responsibility than the people.

Democracy is one of branch of politics. It is the people choice method. It is a best method of government if people elect a good candidate.

India is a one of the largest and well-known democratic countries in world. Party's existences are more than hundreds. New, new parties are coming up now and then with varieties of concept and ideology. Some are National parties and some are regional parties. Now Regional parties are stronger than National parties. Without the help of regional parties, no national parties could be able to form government at Centre for the last so many years. Religious and caste feeling are more exploited in the present Indian democratic system.

The present democratic system may be good on one angle, but may not be better in some other angle. It may be good for some people but not better for all; it may be good for politicians, but not better for country. Happy about having democratic government based on parties system but is it free from corruption, nepotism and maladministration?

Pleasure to have parties elected representatives, but is it free from violence, misuse of power and treats? Is it justice available for all people? Is it not money power and political power are playing major role in this parties democratic system? Is it all police forces are in order and serving for the society without any motive and interest? Is it all judges are delivering proper judgments in time? Are they not influenced by parties' political power and money power? No doubt those educational institutions are improving the standard of education but are they not after money? There is no doubt that medical facilities have tremendously improved in India but are they not exploiting peoples?

We are happy about having parties' democratic government at central as well as at states. But are we happy about their performance? Ruling party declares their achievement, opposition party object and finds faults with it. People have no voice to say anything about their faults but only have to vote alternatively without any choice. But we find no party is free from corruption, nepotism and maladministration.

Without corruption no government can exist may be true. But we cannot accept that corruption alone is the aim of major part of the governments that too in democracy.

There require remarkable developments on infrastructure and other amenities for all the people like other advanced countries. Equal justice is not so easily available for common people in India. Money power and political power are playing major role Even in this party democratic system.

Even Judges and Law and order people are under influence of political and money power. Everyone wants to become rich by any means and wants to be popular among society and wants to have power to dominate others.

Now by way of election we are electing MPs and MLAs to form Government and do five year service for us. But the candidates Who are contesting in the election is not our choice but left to the Party's choice.

From them we have to select the candidates and vote. As of now Democracy is of peoples' government. We are thing that we are only electing the people to serve us. The real fact is something else, because we have to vote for the candidates which are already selected by the parties. We have no other choice. Majority people do not know the candidates name and background. Majority people do not know whether the candidate is without criminal activities.

We are seeing only which party he belongs and then vote for him. Vote for the symbols only. Are we doing correct thing? Is it correct democracy? The elected people concentrate to serve the party than to society.

4

NEW THOUGHT ON DEMOCRACY

Now Medias, Newspapers and Journals are dominating in our everyday life. All are seeing the TV and watching the news and reading the newspapers and magazine and understand day to day affairs and happenings in the world.

Most of them are reading the News papers. Peoples come to know all happenings immediately. People are aware of local and national party politics, the policies of various parties, their capacities, strength and weakness.

Illiteracy has gone mostly, all knows reading and writing. All voters can read the candidates name, face and vote. All are using mobile phone and know the operations.

So there is no need of any symbol now. People can read the candidates name or face and vote.

Present party democratic system is not giving any opportunity for the voters to select and elect the candidates of their choice.

Selection of the candidates is left with party choice. Candidates are selected by each party to contest in election. So this system needs to be changed.

Candidates shall be selected on common and merit basis. They shall be well aware of worldly knowledge. They should be very shrewd and active without any religious, caste and language feeling. People shall elect their representatives among these candidates.

At this juncture people have to think that, are political parties needed for electing MLAs and MPs? Are political parties needed to form government? Do political parties have to rule us instead of collective individual? Why not all these candidates can be independent candidates with some political knowledge and experience.

Without parties also we can conduct election and select the candidates and form government to rule the country. It is very simple and easy also. We are now electing a candidate for our constituency on the basis of some reason. He will be from some party we may know him or may not know him.

He may be from our constituency or may be outsider. But we are selecting him as an MLA or MP by way of party's performance.

After the election if his party is not getting two third majorities, he may fall in opposition party, at that time he can't do anything for the people and constituency which he was elected.

The voting becomes waste here. Parties are formed nowadays based on so many reasons. There are so many parties exist in each state. People's welfare is our motive, people's growth is our motto, and clean government is our intention is the thing they claim. But reality is different; they can't follow what they declare. Even in their party there will be lot of infighting, difference of opinions, aversion which leads to murder and illegal activities. With the support of the party and its name, injustice, suppression, violation of law and orders, corruption are growing. There should be an end to all these immoral activities.

There should be an alternative for this party system. We need a real democracy.

What is the way to get real democracy? First of all we have to select our own known candidates from our own constituency. For this election commission has to conduct written examination among the eligible candidates and select only 15 fresh candidates for each constituency to contest in election.

The candidate shall be of the same constituency. The educational Qualification shall be minimum any degree from the Indian recognized university. Age limit shall be of 25 to 70 for MLAs and MPs. First of all those who wants to contest in election should undergo written examination conducted by respective election commission and come within 15th rank.

So there is no need of parties. This kind of system will eliminate all kinds of problem in the real democracy. It will eliminate unnecessary thinking of entering into politics. Only capable and deserving people can only enter into main political career that will be a real democratic system.

This kind of politics will eliminate caste, creed, region, religion involvement. People can elect good candidates as per their choice. Why two third majority of a single party needed to form a government and to rule the country. Now en number of parties is existing and new parties are launched every now and then. In this situation getting two third majorities for a single party is very difficult in future. Nowadays parties are attracting people to vote based on caste, religion and money.

So that individual candidates is the only better choice for the election, without any party system.

All the elected candidates are eligible to involve in the government and to look after welfare of the people who have elected them.

5

PRESENT PARTY DEMOCRACY

There are no doubts that Indian democracy is governed by the Indian political parties. There are more than hundreds of parties in India consists of National parties and regional parties.

All these parties are selecting their own candidates and contesting in election and may win or lose the seat. Party who gets two third majorities or the Party who can mobilize two third majorities will form the government. Prime Minister, cabinet Ministers and state ministers are decided by the party high commands in case of central government.

Mostly it is left with one man acceptance and concurrence that is party president. Party leader is the fore most supreme authority in that party. Love, affection, interest, loyalty, dependability, obedience, courage and confidence are needed only for the followers. Party workers should not expect these things from the party leader. All power, decision and interest rest with only party leaders.

He can appoint, remove and shift any minister, anybody from any post at any time.

He can make his house servant also to a big position and the same time his so called right hand has a beggar. So elected MPs and MLAs as of now cannot handle anything independently and execute of his own.

First of all he is not allowed to think freely of his own and express his own view in public. All should be under party direction. If he started think of his own he will be immediately removed from the party by stating that he is doing anti party activities. Everything is controlled by party and party executives. In the present party democratic setup the elected representatives have no freedom of thought and action. They have to beg and bow to the party leader for the post.

Party declares election manifesto, which they may fulfill or may not fulfill after winning, but people believe that promise and vote. If it is a real democracy the elected representative shall excise his full powers. He shall have freedom of thoughts, action and do something for his people who have elected him. Now majority of MLAs and MPs are not visiting their constituency because they can't do anything to their constituency without party leaders support. They can't demand the party leader for that, if they demand next day they will be removed from that post.

As of now no Minister, MLA or MP putting their achievement in the banners only parties advertising. So there should be system that a person belonging to that constituency should get power to develop his constituency and get name.

For that Prime Minister, Chief Ministers all others Ministers shall be elected by the elected representatives and all the elected ministers should excise their full powers in his department and he cannot be removed just like that. He can be removed only if the assembly or parliament approved by the voting system.

Local public have to give their manifesto to the candidates who stands in election and get his concurrence before voting instead of candidates giving manifesto. This requires new democratic system.

6

POLITICAL PARTIES AND THEIR CONDITION IN INDIA

"Parties are like fort and Leaders are like king"

Indians are very much fond of parties. Each Indian wants to be a leader and leadership position at any cost. In India entering into politics is very easy. If you have enough money you can start a party, and if you start a party somehow money will flow automatically. People will come and join your party to get some position, MLA and MP tickets.

People are of the opinion that politics is the easy way of making money. They want importance in society and public. They will spend thousands of rupees to print banners with their photos and display for public to show their significance and importance. This has grown in extreme sense as of now. Every now and then some new parties are launched. Parties are based on some policies, based on castes, based on religions, based on regions, based on languages and based on so many reasons.

Some are forming party to protect them from others domination; some are to protect their properties and some are to have safety of their life.

In the party system the Party leader is like a king. He can do anything in his political Party and others are to hold the posts for name sake. Party leader till his death is a monarch. He will have few people along with him as confident and he will chance these person time to time, others will come and go, they will be thrown aside in the name of indicting new faces. During this small tenures the loyal workers or disciples has to earn something to lead their life because most of their life time was sacrificed for the party.

Some innocent party followers sacrifice their life for the sake of parties, commit crimes and disturb publics and properties. But party leaders are always in safe and intact, leading the royal life even if they are in power or not. But party leaders are always keen only on growth of their party, for that they are ready to do anything to attract the public in such a way to come to the power.

They may not fully interest in growth of the country, economy, poverty and unemployment problem. They give free thing to catch masses.

Leader makes people to think that he is the only person doing favor to the people than his party people and others. In such a big country, having so many big states, people believe only one person, the Party Leader and costing their votes rather than believing the candidates capacities. Really it is pathetic. Majority of the party leaders' sons, daughters and relatives will be the only hires of his party leadership and party valuable positions. They will plan such a way that their family members only will become or hold the leadership. Without doing any job the whole family will enjoy the high life style, comforts with fame and popularity and govern the people and country.

Party funds, government money and people tax money or black money are the sources for their enjoyment. We can see the all India scenarios, all the parties from where they are getting money for their expenses.

It is only from the party funds or some way other government money; all are nothing but our tax money. Party fund is collected by the party followers. Some followers, they will give their own money to the party, in turn the party will help them to earn more money than their contributions.

They will collect from big business people, rich people and from small vendors also. If you really see all these money are people tax money, black money or from the government revenue.

Otherwise who will spend from their pockets? Is the party leader will spend from his pocket or minister will spend from his pocket? How much government money and peoples' money, tax money is spend for party leader birthday, facilitation and their comfort living. How many political parties are there in India? To maintain their party's how much money is needed, how much vehicles are needed, how many party head Quarters are needed and so on. All these hundreds of Indian political party's expenses will be more than our annual India budget.

In such situation is the party system needed in India? Can't we select MLAs and MPs without party system? If we select and elect MLAs and MPs of our own choice without party system we can save lacs and lacs of crores and save the country from poverty and unemployment problem.

We need not get any free thing from government or subsidy from government. We need not believe false promises of the party's and vote for them with some expectations. Why should we beg them for free things and price control. They are making us or the common public really poor and poorer.

Still if we believe party system, even after thousands of year the Poverty line will remain as such. So we have to come out of party system and elect our own known people in our area for our development. First we have to see our area development and our growth, our area people development and growth. If each area grows the entire country automatically will grow. Nobody will demand separate state or area and there won't be any violence on area dispute. All the people demand will be met automatically. We need not worry about other areas growth.

We need not worry who is the Prime Minister or Chief Minister, if we elect a good MPs or MLAs, they will elect good Prime Minister and Chief Minister.

So we need a real new democracy and keep this old party democracy out.

7

MLAS AND MPS CANDIDATES' SELECTION IN THE PARTY SYSTEM

With the help of Top leaders, the party leaders select the candidates to contest for MLAs and MPs with some special criteria keeping in mind. Those candidates who offer more will get tickets. Candidate may be qualified or not, may not to be capable or shrewd, but he should be time being candidate not the permanent candidates.

Few leaders and few permanent candidates are constant and others will be thrown out in the disguise of introducing new faces in each election. Some loyal persons who work day and night for the party and sacrifice their life also will be thrown out just like that. After getting humiliation and ill treatment, got much vexed will be slowly going away from the party. But party and party leader will not bother about that person, but will get rid of him by accusing him in some other way. Individual man can't do anything in the party system.

New people those who are coming to the party may not know their future fate but they will work as they are the only loyal worker for the party and party leaders.

But one thing is true that all are joining and working for the party to earn money, power and fame. Some people future will become bright, someone else will be short, someone will be long and someone will be too long. Party has three layer workings system, lower, middle and top.

Lower level is like soldier in the war field who has to do whatever their captain says sacrifices and die. This lower level is for fighting, protecting or organizing. They will be purchased sometimes for doing some political activities and party work.

Middle level will be the co coordinator between Top and Bottom. Top level only always take decision and run the party. Top level gives instruction to the middle level. Middle level has to face a lot of challenges, threats, lose their properties and sacrifice their life to keep up the party in alive and intact.

Party leader will have alliance with other parties as per his convenience and he may change his policy as per the present situation, but party works should be always loyal to him.

If anybody criticize his action then he be branded as person doing anti party activities and will be thrown out of the party. Party leaders should get the shares from his deputies. Without sharing and supporting the way to share may not go along with him for long time.

8

MLAS AND MPS CANDIDATES' SELECTION IN THE NEW DEMOCRACY

In the new democratic system the candidates are independent candidates. Need not to offer anything to anybody to get the election seat. He needs not to beg anybody for the MLA or the MP seat. Only thing is that he has to pass the examination conducted by the election commission and rank within 15th.He is the candidate not a leader but has no permanent followers.

He is confined to his constituency only. He can have his confidents' followers to protect him and work for him. But he can't build blind followers like the political party doing as of now. For him the area is limited, support also will be limited, genuine people only will support him. Here he can't give false promise to his own native people. Whatever promises if he gives he has to fulfill that, if he got elected?

Otherwise he may not be elected for the next time. If he is elected he is a free man, he need not worry even about other Ministers, Chief Minister, Prime Minister and others, because he is not elected under anybody support and under anybody pressure and courtesy. He will have all freedom of thought and action to fight for the growth of his area and bring so many facilities and benefits to his constituency.

He needs not worry about Chief Minister, Prime Minister other ministers and others. Nobody is his boss so also for all MLAs and MPs. He needs not earn to give party fund or party workers and party higher ups, so he may not do more financial damage to the society and government.

Enthusiasm, interest, joy and rejuvenation will be there in the New Democratic system. There will be a chance for en number of people to contest for a single constituency. Interestingly to avoid this problem, candidates in that constituency have to write an examination and contest election as said above. Here all are independent candidates only.

9
CANDIDATES SYMBOLS IN THE ELECTION

Present party democratic system the symbol is kept to identify the candidate to vote. It is party identification rather than the candidate. It is a good and wonderful system for illiterate and less educated people to vote without any difficulty.

During independence the numbers of parties are less and it was easy for the election commission to allot the symbols. After the 70 years of the independence there is remarkable change in education and awareness of the people. Life standard, living style and dressing senses has changed a lot.

All branches of education making enormous impact in India. Considering all these fact eliminating the symbols and introducing a new system may be better for the people and there will be warm welcome for this act. In New Democratic system there is no party, no leader and therefore no need of symbol. Since all are individual candidates, the symbol shall be of candidate's passport size photos with his name. Considering the fact that mostly all are educated and the availability of Medias may train the masses for the election procedures and system, it can be taken as granted that people can vote by identifying the face of the candidates even not able to read the name.

So the symbol will be his name with his passport size photo. Since the candidates are familiar to them, people will know them better by name and figure and vote for the better candidates. It is purely people choice, and better candidate will perform better manner.

10

ADVANTAGES OF
THE PARTY SYSTEM

Single party wins majority seats in central election or state election, it can form a stable government and the advantages are as follows.

The party leader will have all the powers; he can select the ministers and other officials as per his choice and run the government without any hindrance. As a single man he can take quick decision and execute.

He can do all the state developmental work without any interruption. He can change the non-cooperative, non-performance officials, ministers and others for the better performance of the government. He can strengthen the industries, infrastructures, create employment opportunities, solve religious problem, brings communal harmony and peace among people. He can give good education and also develop the agriculture, which is more neglected field as of now.

As a country man he can improve foreign policy, have good relationship with other countries for import and export trade activities, for the infrastructure improvement, science and technology development, higher education and employment opportunities. He can protect our country from other countries aggression and invasion.

11
DISADVANTAGES OF THE PARTY SYSTEM

There are numerous disadvantages in the single party power. The single man, party leader if he take wrong policy and decision all the above items will get spoiled. With his personnel ego he will not follow the policy and plan of the earlier government.

He will make another plan and policy to suit his party agenda. This will lead a huge loss for the government.

If he is a vindictive nature he will be always thinking that how to spoil the other party and party leaders. For this he will be spending more time than running the government. Moreover Party leader can't satisfy all, so he will be increasing his opponents whom in turn will be dangerous for his government and his life. If he is assassinated there will be turmoil in the country, even if has natural death then also there will be trouble in the country.

Violence looting, fighting, murders and destruction of public and private property will take place. Sometime party leader can take wrong decision others may not object him, by which there will be a lot of financial loss for the country.

Single man policy is dangerous for the country. If this national party leader says anything, anywhere it will have more value and it will reflect from one end of the country to another end. If he is insulted in Kashmir, Kanniakumari will burn, if he or his party wins in Kanniakumar, there will be a celebration in Kashmir.

This is a huge loss for our country. Some national party may not be having good policy and leaders but to form a stable government people have to vote for that party, which again is not a correct voting.

Majority Indian people believes in traditional voting, vote for the same party whatever may be the reason, vote for the same family whatever may be the reasons. Nowadays single national party is not winning the majority seats so that they have alliance with some other parties to form a government.

In that situation the government can't take any decision freely and not able to run freely. Corruption, Maladministration, misuse of power will take place.

Even in single party rule this will happen freely since all the powers are with them. They can have collusion with medias, news channels, capitalists, judiciary, law and order and election commission or they will suppress all of them for their victory.

As of now we are noticing that parliament and assembly is not functioning without disturbance. MPs and MLAs are sometime not allowing the proceedings. They are stopping the proceeding of the Lok Sabha and Rajya Sabha.

Opposition parties stating that the ruling parties are doing mistakes, Ruling parties stating that opposition parties are making unnecessary demands. Opposition parties say that they are fighting for truth to come out.

But ruling party with its majority makes everything nil. Both show their party strength in the parliament rather than solving the problem.

But in assembly opposition has less voice. They will not be allowed to speak. This becomes a mockery of democracy. If all are individual candidates they realize the importance and abide the rules. In the party democratic system each one wants to protect their own party, party leader and party people first, then the next is to project that whatever their party doing is correct.

This is clearly evident from the act of politicians are speaking contrary to his previous statement and changing his statement time to time. Changing over his alliance from one party to another and justifying their acts.

Without the non-co-operation of the parliamentarians government has to lay down some good project, drop some good policies or has to pass some unwanted bills.

12

ADVANTAGES OF
THE PARTY LESS SYSTEM

The disadvantage of party less system is less than party democratic system, but advantages are more and more.

Here all the winners are participating in the government. In party democratic system to pass the bill two third majorities required.

The ruling party member has to compulsorily vote even if does not like the bill. This is party compulsion. It is against his conscious.

In the new democratic system two third of the ruling member itself have to vote to pass the bill or against the bill. This is real democracy. Here individuals are fighting for election, no collusion so there is no caste and religious influence. Other advantages are expressed in all other chapters.

13

UNREST IN PARLIAMENT AND LEGISLATIVE ASSEMBLY

Country is in rest but Parliament is in unrest; streets are calm but Assembly is in storm. Parliament has to be considered as the most respected gathering hall and most decision making hall in calm atmosphere. Today parliament is adjoined for three times, four times or completely due to opposition's demands and disturbances.

There are kayos in Parliament and could not function properly in the so valuable parliament session. **It becomes air conditioned playground for the elected representatives.**

This is because of so many reasons and mistakes between ruling parties and oppositions.

Sometimes it is ruling parties' negligence, sometimes it is opposition parties' demands. Voted people are helpless to solve this problem and they are only the spectators to watch the fun fares in TV, laugh and enjoy. People who are the supporters of the ruling party will boil and opposition party will justify.

Why all these things are happening and how to bring an end to this kind of activities of the parliamentarians. Each parliamentarian of the opinion that they are doing genuine and it is for the welfare of people and country.

Both sides are strong enough to demonstrate. But where they are getting such a strong support to do such disturbance in parliament and assembly? Is it outcome of the party strength and support? Is it on individual outcry? If all are independent MLAs/MPs can they disturb parliament or assembly proceedings? Or they create such unruly situation either in parliament or in assembly?

Corruption, misuses of powers, favoritism and unwanted criticism, statement are becoming the basic issues for the unrest in parliament and assembly.

Individual parliamentarian can't make lacs and lacs of crores loss for government, will not do huge corruption, will not misuse his power and will not do favoritism, unwanted criticism and statement.

He will abide by rules and regulation and allow to parliament or assembly to function peacefully. With the support of parties only all the above mistakes are happening.

14

HOW PEOPLE
ARE VOTING NOW

"Voting is a wise thing, but mostly it becomes regrets for us in this party democratic system"

Interest and enthusiasm surface into the hearts and minds of the people's during election time. Money, honey and wine are poured on people during election by the parties, so that people started making use of this situation presently.

Dreams are common to bring a major change in election. Some are more vigorous to defeat some party; some are with more interest to vote for some party. Some are lazy about the election saying that as an unwanted one. Some are in dilemma as to whom to vote. People are bound to vote for party's selected candidates only. People are voting based on election propaganda, party's performance, likes and dislikes.

Some people are voting for the same party irrespective of their performance whatever may be the national problems. Some people are voting for the changes. Some people are voting only to give majority to form government.

Some people are voting on the castes basis. Some are voting for free benefits. Some are voting for money. People are voting based on so many reasons. Public below poverty line are mostly exploited group, they expect free thing, so many benefits from the government, so they vote based on the party's promises.

Some are loyal worker or group for the particular party so that they will vote for that party only. Some are voting for the alternate government whatever may be the reason even if the present government policy and performance are good.

Some will vote at that movement what they think. Most of the people voting for the symbols only, not knowing the candidate name and not seen his photos also. Some people are brain washed and misdirected by the speech of the political leaders during election. Some people are not really satisfied by the present government so they will vote for other party. Some people do not like family domination so that they will vote for others.

Those people who are not getting any benefit and envy of other people enjoying the benefit vote for others. Some people will not at all vote but blame the government performance. Some people are not at all voting but speak politics and blame the government performance.

Those people who are not voting in election are not having any rights to talk politics and blame governments. Those people who are so lazy to spend two hours in a five year tenure is not fit to blame anybody and not ask any benefit from government. They are not fit to be a citizen.

In the ex-ordinary circumstance only one has to miss voting, but not all the time purposefully. 20 to 30 percent of the people are not voting, if they vote there will be winning chance for some candidates.

Mostly people expect so many profitable things from the government. Even highly income groups also expect so many benefits from the government. It is the fault of the all parties; it is a creation of all parties; they declare some benefits and free things in their election manifesto in order to get votes. If they win elections they have to fulfill their manifestos for that money have to be siphoned from somewhere else.

In the other election opposition party will declare more benefits and free things than the ruling party, so people will vote for the opposition party.

People are seeing the benefits only. Even if you give everything as free, people will never get satisfaction. Politician polluted the people mind, now people are polluting the politicians' mind. The result is our tax money only getting wasted in different form. But poor people are thinking that it is free from government.

In the **New Democratic System**, thought on voting will differ. All will come forward to vote.

There won't be NOTA voting. There will be enormous interest among masses for voting. The candidates will be known to them, dear and near to them. People may not expect money from the candidates instead they will vote for betterment. Money, honey and wine are poured on people during election by the parties, so that people started making use of this situation presently. This may not be there in **new democracy election**.

15

STATE AND CENTRAL GOVERNMENTS – RELATIONSHIP

Coordination and good relationship needed between state and central government.

Strained relationship, disinterested nature, uninterested behavior, emotional and egoistic nature on both sides will affect the industrial developments of the states and overall countries growth in agriculture, education, employment, environment, health and economy.

Some of the states will have lot of resources like ores, minerals, and waters, the excess shall be shared among other states. Some states will be dry and depend upon on other states for waters. The favorable and amicable relationship among states and central are the only solution to solve these problems.

This is mainly in the hands of the political parties and some organization. Nowadays people are instigated and inculcated the feeling of religion, language and statehood, which are the root cause for the unrest and mass agitation. People are electing regional parties for their state and national parties for the central. People want a stable government at the central whatever may be the reason. They do not want to vote again and again so they are voting some better party. If elected regional party is not have good relationship with that national party, whatever help the state government asks may be delayed or denied.

If both are in good relation everything will be normal and smooth. Nowadays people are voting for regional parties that is their own state parties rather than the national parties, because they think that regional parties is better for them and it will concentrate more on them than the national parties. They can easily approach the government for any problem.

Suppose they vote for national party and elected to power, the national party leader only decide the Chief Minister for that state, who will be the outsider of that state sometimes. People are not in favor this kind of politics.

In the same way if regional party comes to the power the regional party leader only will decide who will be the Chief Minister and other Ministers.

If **new democracy system** is implemented the elected members only will elect the Chief Minister and other

Ministers. It is a pure democratic way. Chief Minister and other Minister will be elected based on the potential, capacity and knowledge. All elected member will be responsible for the selection of the Chief Minister and Minister. All the elected MLAs have strong role and responsibility to elect a good Chief Minister and Ministers. In the same way the Chief Minister and other minister bound to listen and act to all the elected Members (MLAs). The party leader monarch system will not be there.

16

INTER STATES – RELATIONSHIP

States to states should also have a cordial relationship among them for better sharing of resources and projects implementation. If both states have common boundary still they should have more understating and lovable relationship. If any misbehavior, misunderstanding, wrong policy, provoking statement will affect the boundary people first.

Such kinds of problems we have witnessed so many in our country. These problems are arising due to the political parties and some organizations support and instigation. Supports are coming forward boldly because they have strength, money and might.

If we follow the **New Democracy**, such thing will never happen in any of the state. All will live peacefully. There won't be any suppression of the people. There will not be any leader to start such kind of agitation. Caste politics, religious politics, language politics and son of the soil politics will not work. Border line living people will have both the state culture and language feeling. This may be viewed in border sense. All are human beings they will have their own tastes and interest. There should not be any compulsion on people to learn particular language and practice particular religion. Even a small issue which is flaring up now and then and bring tension among states will be nullified.

17
STATE POLITICS

There are 29 states and 7 union territories in our country. Each state and union territory has their own government headed by their elected party. In totality each state government will have major responsibility and role for its own state development.

But respective MPs and MLAs should have major role and involvement for their respective areas development.

In our present party democracy system respective MPs and MLAs recommends and put forth the demands to their party higher cadres only after by the public pressure.

This will be studied by the party and final decision will be given. At any cost the elected representative can't freely open their month and express their view without their party concern in parliament or in assembly. They will speak only as per party written statement and not of their own or individually.

They have no freedom of speech and action. If they want any development or benefits for their constituency they have to approach party, party has to permit and do the things and finally party will earn more credit than the elected members. Elected members are at the mercy of their party and party leader ship. If a member is very close to his party leader he can do anything. Neutralization of self-respect is common factor or a major tool for the successive prolonging tenure.

In the **New Democratic System** all the above deficiency will be taken care of. MPs and MLAs will have full freedom of speech and action.

They are not depending upon anybody for their action. They can recommend and execute the project, do welfare measure and get credit.

18

JUDICIARY

Delayed judgments are denied justice. Normally getting judgments takes long time. Is it due to insufficient courts, lawyers, advocates and judges or increasing number of cases? Is it money given more importance than the judgment? The reasons are not yet so clear. Some cases are prolonging for decades.

But judiciary is respected always because it is the final authority in our democratic system.

Even it is wrong judgment or one sided, people has to accept it. Judge may be a corrupt; lawyer may be corrupt but no other go we have to accept their verdict. It is a court of law we have created and accepted. The most affected are poor people and helpless ones. Disrespecting the court of law, nobody is above the law is an umbrella to whom? Lawyers earn money by extending the cases; judges are also part for that.

There is no time limit to fish the cases. Advocates and lawyers are openly supporting some political parties and have party membership.

So they have to support some political parties and will be influenced by the political parties. Judges are also human beings so naturally afraid of political pressure, rich people and rowdyisam.

Only poor and helpless people are punished, politicians and rich people escape from the severe punishments; lawyers and judges are planning in such way to favor the judgment.

In **New Democracy System** judges, advocates and Lawyers will not have any political pressure, because there won't be any party masses to threaten them.

They get their due promotion and transfer without political interference. They can work freely without any interference. They can freely argue their cases and give fair judgment without any fear. They can finish the cases within the stipulated time. The number of cases will automatically degrease. Corruption, robbery, murder case will be minimum.

19

LAW AND ORDER

Law and orders are under the control of police department. If they perform their duty perfectly there won't be any law and order problems. Society will be living in peace. Daily there is news of so many robberies and murders.

What may be the reason? After robbery and murder the investigation starts what is the use? Where is the law and order? Why we can't control it even after so many incidents? But there is no correct solution yet. But law and Order department concentrate more on government directions; they follow and obey the order of the present government first.

If the present government says to arrest a particular person they have to arrest him by creating some false records. To raid somebody's house they have to raid. This is their duty.

But government will say that it is a measure of action to suppress corruption and to maintain law and order. Other than this authoritarianism, corruption in this department is common. For filing the case we have to give bribe, for further proceeding the case we have to give bribe to each and every person in the police station, for withdrawing the case also we have to give bribe. What police are justifying is that they did not get enough salary and enough fund for the investigation. Police can torture the innocent peoples also under the influence of money and power rather than the real criminal. Police are sometimes compelled to act under the influence of money, political power and rowdysam.

They have to file the case in such a way that the case will go in favor of the person whom they want to help. Moral and ethics are out of fashion now. They also want promotion, transfers and earn money and property within short period. Moreover they can't be honest in this present social environment, where people are so selfish, not bother about truth and justice. Ego and prestige influences everybody more than the tolerance and forgiveness. Traffic police in the road side openly doing the illegal collections and says politicians wants, higher ups wants the money.

They preferred location postings to earn money, for that transfer they are paying lakhs and lakhs to higher ups. In public and in duty they earn more respect but in society people have more conscious to have relationship with them. Perfection we need but not perfection to perfection. Perfection is an infinitive; comparison may give ever ending conclusion.

What may purify the system? What is needed for some perfection? Who has the responsibility, Public, society, politicians, employee, individual or anybody? The answer is all are responsible. All are lacking in their responsibility but blaming other sides. Let us analyses how the **New Democratic System** will rectify these.

First of all there won't be any political pressure or party's involvement on their day to day work. Higher police officer will excise their power real without any political interference do justice to the public. Higher ups will have more responsibility and have to answer if there is failure in the law and order system to only one local elected leader, not for all party leaders.

Unnecessary shifting of higher police officers will not take place and their Postings and transfers will be departmental level not political level. Since all elected members are in ruling party they will concentrate on law and order and protect the people fromrobbery and murder. People will get justice. Law and order people will not indulge in unlawful activities in collusion with politicians and criminals. Law and order will be in favor of people not in favor of some selected political parties.

20

ELECTION COMMISSION

Duty of the election commission is to conduct fair and free election to elect MLAs and MPs once in five years. In the present political set up election commission claims that they are conducting fair and free election. But many fields are not under their control and also they are bound to favor some party and some people.

They can't touch some people and powerful party candidates. They are under the merry of government, they also require promotion, transfers and earn money and property in short term. During the election, the election commission is not able to screen the candidates properly, not able to control both capturing and illegal voting.

They are not able to totally control the money transaction, money power and muscle power. But for record sake they maintain some records. During election if some violation happens electoral officers also helpless and some election commissioner says that it is beyond their control. They are also under some political threats and influence.

In the **New Democracy** setup the election commission will conduct real fair and free election. Election will be conducted once in five years only without by election. In this system no need of by election, if MP seat fall vacant it is prime minister responsibility to take care of that constituency if MLA seat vacant it is the responsibility of chief minister to care of that constituency.

There will not be any political party influence and money influence during election. Individual candidates cannot mobilize so strength to do any illegal activities like booth capturing and illegal voting during election. Individual candidate can't offer so much money to the public to get votes. There is no pressure like that an individual party has to win with two third majority. All elected persons will be part of the government. So People peacefully will vote and elect the MPs and MLAs. By this system no one seek election commission favoritism.

21
ELECTIONS

During elections there are thousands of functions. There are big, bigger and biggest banners, towering posters, attractive paintings, wonderful pictures, wall write-ups will be seen everywhere. Leaders will glitter around glittering colourful florescent lights. Party leaders will be predominant in posters and candidates will be next in size. Symbol will be alone signifying its importance. Symbol is more important and worthier than candidates and manifesto. But now it is controlled somehow. But money is flowing like river everywhere.

All parties are spending huge amount which was legally and illegally collected one as party funds.

Everywhere in party meetings the leaders will address the gatherings about his party performance, achievements and other party failures and lacunas'. One leader will criticize the other leader and bring laughter in gatherings.

There will be interesting and enthusiastic speeches among party leaders and party workers. Thousands of lights will glow, thousands of stereos will echo, there will be dance and singing. Party leader will have cyclonic visit to gather votes, candidates will visit extensively to the nook and corner of the places and canvass for votes. People will be waiting to defeat some party and bring another party for power. Some people will be in dilemma saying whichever party comes nothing going to improve. Some will murmur and say that all are not good, not worried about people and country but will gather money for themselves and their parties.

This kind of situation and displeasure is common during elections. One way it is a good, income for those involved in this election work. Some amount of black money is coming out and spent for some purpose.

At least some money is circulated among people. It is one way of healthy sign should not require any restriction.

Certainly we can believe that the party less system of government will be better. It will eliminate majority of the democratic defects which are exists now. The party democracy is nothing but indirect way of king democracy, it is nothing but defeating one king by another king once in five years. It needs elimination at this stage. Election commission can conduct free and fair election. Local people will automatically eliminate the criminal contesting in election.

The absence of the political parties will pay a good way for the functioning of the any government body either it is election commission, judiciary, police department or railways and so on. Election commission can take independent decision, and conduct the real free and fair election. Only qualified local persons can stand in the election with the help of their local people. He makes Familiarization with the local people, and then only he will be elected in election.

Unknown person cannot come and contest in the election as like in the present system.

22

BOOTH CAPTURING & EVM TAMPERING

During election based on some people, or some parties' instruction, booths are captured and illegal voting is done to win in the election. Nowadays EVM is tampered or replaced. Here money power, party power and muscle power play major factor. This kind of action is not able to control totally even after so many rules and regulations. This is happening due to victory of particular candidates to get party majority.

In the **New Democracy** there will be no place for such kind of activities and it will be controlled easily by the election commission. There will be no mass to do such activities. There is no party and party workers to organize and do such activities. No state level or central level connection or co-ordination will be there for this booth capturing or EVM tampering and replacing activities.

It is not necessary, since no majority is required to form the government; all those elected are the ruling party. So voting will be peaceful. Police can control the entire situation normally and people can vote without any fear.

23
MONEY POWER

Parties are ruthlessly collecting money from business peoples, trades, and rich people for their election expenses. Even small traders and business men are not spared. Some capitalists are giving fund to the party which are supporting their business. Common people and poor people cannot understand this kind of politics.

Now in all elections money power plays a major factor and nullify the people mind for time being and getting the votes. Some parties throwing money like anything to the common people and achieve their goals. At the same time crores of money poured on local medias and newspapers as well as outside of the country to promote that party as doing wonderful thing. **If new democracy comes, without party system**, individual candidates cannot afford such expenses and money power play will be mostly nil. Business peoples, trades, rich people do not worry about the party harassment for fund collection. Rich people, business people, big factory owners and other traders can pay their real tax and get away from harassments.

24
EDUCATION

What is the fate of Government educational institution now in all states? There is no proper building, proper teaching staff, proper laboratory, proper toilet facility, proper drinking water facility, proper play-ground for children in most of the government institutions. While ruling the party will not take proper steps to improve the facilities and education standards, but while coming to the opposition they will highlight all this points.

All these state government institutions are having their mother tongue as their teaching language. They are compelling other state students also to learn their mother tongue. This is may be their strong attachments towards their mother tongue and other reason is that they want to grow their party by inculcating sentiment of language feeling among the masses. Most of the people want their children to learn English to earn livelihood. But in public they show more attachment for their mother tongue.

The standard of education needs improvement in some of the government institution. Private institutions are doing well than the government institutions. Only people who are not able to offered the private school fee and expenses are sending their children to government school.

This is because children are shining in education and getting good discipline in private institution than the government institution. No MLAs and MPs visiting government schools, colleges and analyzing the reason for failure to coup the standard equal to private institutions. But their part ends with attending some functions and there also they will speak about their party achievements and praise their party leader rather than the importance of the education.

Government institutions employees are well paid than the private institution, but could not bring much standard because of some lacuna which government failed to solve.

In the **new democratic system** the elected representatives bound to visit all the institution and do betterment activities. He can get funds or fight for the funds to develop his area educational institutions. He is not depending upon any body, any minister and any party leadership to throw him out. Government institutions will come up in standard and private institutions also will get equal pay. Otherwise the opposition candidates can highlight the failures and activate the causes. This kind of provision is not there in the party democracy.

25

EMPLOYMENT

At present the state government is doing the job recruitment by the limited employment exchange. They are not in position to concentrate on individual constituency. This is not giving any fruitful justification for all those job seekers. The central government also follows some method and doing the recruitment. All these are not able to give full employment opportunity to all and satisfy all.

Government has to incur lot of expenses than the profit. Salary, perks and maintenance are the major expanses for any government. But government can easily control and manage these situations. In the name of free education the education standard are not improving along with private institution. In the name of free medical the treatment are not able to coup on par with private medical. Actually government is doing injustice to some section of the people.

Moreover under party system people have to elect some party to form government even if they have unemployment problem and poverty problem. So government is not much bothered about those kinds of problems. They only concentrate on building up their party, party system and attracting the vote bank masses.

In the **new democratic system** respective MLA and MP have enough freedom to concentrate on their own constituency and solve the unemployment problem in a spaced manner. They can create job opportunity in the field of agriculture, education, transport, government offices, municipalities, factories and trade centers. Each constituency can create an employment centre and easily solve the problem.

New democratic system will solve most of the unemployment problem. For those who are highly qualified and capable of getting employment somewhere we need not worry. For those who are less qualified and not able to get employment anywhere we can create employment in so many fields in the constituency itself. They can concentrate on improving the education standard and medical facilities without any hindrance.

26
AGRICULTURAL GROWTH

Worldwide all countries are depend upon agricultural. Without agriculture there is no food. Some countries which cannot produce agricultural products depend upon other countries. India is an agricultural country all well aware of it. India is a self sufficient country in agricultural production.

It is exporting many agricultural products. Still majority of the Indian farmers are living in poverty and meet only hand to mouth. Most of the time there is no proper rain in seasons, continuous draughts, sometimes heavy rain spoil the crops. Insecticide problems, insufficient water, scarcity of fertilizers, poor quality of fertilizers, exorbitant rate of fertilizers, and non-availability of labors are so many constraints farmers are facing.

Small farmers may not able to do agriculture since they faces so many losses. Small farmers are committing suicides since they cannot repay the debts and bear the losses. Still agricultural problem is not fully solved. There is always interstate water sharing problem. Each state is ruled by separate party. Each state has to concentrate on their agricultural production. So Coordination among them may not be possible always. Union Government cannot always interfere and solve the interstate water problem. Even though there is existence of the agreement between states in water sharing, sometimes they may not agree to share because of their own state people pressure. Doing agriculture is a mean job, for the present young generation.

Even less education person feel hesitant to do the agricultural work. People work in mechanic shops, construction works and so many labor works but not interested to do agriculture work. But there is a drawback in agricultural work, there is no constant and regular work and income. It is a seasonal work. But we can make this field also as a profitable one by bring so many modifications. There is a plenty of employment opportunity in the agricultural field.

We can create a cooperative society in each village and give required labors, materials, machines and fertilizers for the farmers. During the harvest we can collect the dues we paid for them in the form of grains.

For such an improvement elected representatives has to take steps for the implementation in their respective areas. Now in the present party democratic system elected representatives and officials misuses the funds allotted for the agricultural development. Poor farmer not able to get loans, only landlords are enjoying. Even though government implements so many schemes it is not giving fruitful results.

It is done under party direction, for the credit of the party workers, party people and to fetch the votes.

So that it is not so effective. In the new democratic system we can do wonders in the agricultural field. Like hundred days work in a year government can give free labors for agricultural work. This will help for farmers and agricultural growth.

27

INDUSTRIAL GROWTH

Industrial growth is one of the lead factors for the countries economical growth. With the limited manpower, less investments the production can be achieved to supply in the market for reasonable prices. In this vast land, quality production may fetch the imports and foreign exchange. Industrial growth improves the employment opportunity, thereby improve living standard of the people.

The brain drain will not be there. Most of the Indian, doctors, engineers, specialist and even common people find jobs in other countries and settles there. Once goes there they are not interested to come here since they get more comforts there than here. This is because of the industrial growth happened there.

Our party politics is a major hindrance for our industrial growth. One party will launch a good programme but other party will see that it will be closed. The party ego works not reason. They will explain very good reason to public for its closure.

People also will blindly support. If a ruling party starts a project, that project will not be taken care of by the subsequent ruling party.

This is because of the party domination, one party will not allow the other party to get good name. They not worried about the financial loss or people gain. Inter states object will be there for some project. State and central will not agree for some projects. All are because of political reason. Some government spending unnecessary thing for their promotion.

In **new democratic system** in the absence of political party, the Elected representatives will come for conclusion and execute the project. There won't be any party hindrance there won't be any masses behind for doing things.

Once the project is started it will go on there is no question of stopping or closing. There will be a good prospect for the industrial development. There won't be any favoritism, misuse of power and wastage of property and money. The financial loss will be minimum and profit will become more.

28

RELIGIOUS FEELING

India is not only a multi religious nation but also multi Language and multicultural nation. No country in the world has so many religion and language. But everywhere people are made very sensitive to religion, language and culture by so many ways of practice.

But everybody speaks about tolerance, patience, unity and harmony in India than any other country. Politicians and religious leaders are able to utilize these practice and started playing double roles and exploiting the feeling of the people to achieve their goal. The political parties utilize the feelings of language, religion and caste to win in the election.

Actually people are not much concerned about their religion, language and caste, all the time they concentrate on their livelihood.

People are not interested to insult other religion, fight with other religion and destroy other religion. But international level politics, national politics, international religious organization and national level religious organization are instigating unnecessary doubts into the peoples' mind which results unrest and violence among people. But actually in life we need language to communicate, but need not have religion and caste. But anyhow it was practiced and followed by the ancient traditions so the old and fanatic people not able to come out of it.

All religious people are victim of the sentiments. They blindly believe sentiments forgetting that all religions are teaching the same. There was no religion, language and caste while human beings are started living. Growth of the human beings established countries and languages. Further growth created religions and castes. If everybody understands this concept then all the religious and caste sentiments will die. Now young generation is very positive, they never bothered about religion, caste and language; they started living as they like in this fastest world.

They never want to break their head with old sentiments which give conflict among society. For this the **new democratic system** will pay a way for the communal and religious harmony in national level. There won't be enough connectivity to instigate any religious issues. Elected representative from the respective constituency will be capable of controlling their area. In such circumstances the international level instigation will not work out. Disrespect and enmity on other religion will slowly subside and people will live in calm with dignity and respect. There is no party in state or central level to instigate or support language and religious activities anywhere in the country.

Respective elected representative of that constituency will amicable solve these problem. Moreover religions are created to come out of other domination, to live with freedom as they like, to suit their living area, practice to suit their attitudes and separate people from the common world.

But a man believes one religion there itself he started doing injustice to others religion. Unknowingly started hating others religion. This people are not able to understand. But in the outset they say all regions are equal and there is only one god.

But all regions are making their own religious people as slaves. Without religious practice one cannot do marriage, other functions and funeral. In such a way all religions are indirectly controlling their own people. All are slave for religion and their gods.

Like also caste if a man claims that he belongs to some caste there itself he started hating others. Unknowingly he is creating caste feeling in his blood. Religions are created olden day while people are in poverty, suppression, illiteracy and ignorance. Now after thousands of years why new religion is not coming? Now people are not ready to blindly for new religion. So therefore here after there is no need of any religion and caste.

29

LANGUAGE FEELING

Another factor which was inculcated in the minds of the people is the language feelings. Any language is mainly for the communication. In India there are more than 22 languages, which is spoken and written in practice.

Each one has their own mother tongue. Usually each one will have attachment for their mother tongue. But mother tongue has its own limitation. With the help of mother tongue alone it is very very difficult for us to achieve what we want in this vast world.

There is lot of opportunity to live comfortable in other areas and part of world. So we cannot depend upon one language alone. Even in India we need the help of other languages in day to day work. To do business we need various languages, to study we need the support of other languages, for the employment we have to learn certain languages. Now Indian are going to other countries for employment or they using their tongue? South Indian are going to north India,

North Indian are coming to south India what for but for their livelihood. Because government is not able fulfill their requirement. People are not to believe the false promises of the any government. But they have to live and support their family.

Now Japanese, Chinese and Russian are learning other languages, because they want better communication and understanding of the subject to improve technology, trade and employment that does not mean they disrespect their mother tongue.

Therefore peoples are allowed to learn other languages for their livelihood. There is no need of translation and finding the new words to our mother tongue. We can adopt the same word in to our mother tongue. For that we need not have a language translation committee and waste the time and money. This is not going to bring major change in the field. Now people movements are fast, ready to adopt any style and standards.

They do not want to confine in small area. There should be a language freedom, states, politicians and governments should not restrict students to learn a particular language.

In **new democracy** there won't be any leader to instigate the language feeling, so people will and practice any language as per their will and wish.

30
CASTES

Upto Guptha dynasty there was no distinct caste system exists in India. At that time population was less and they were doing their jobs of their own.

When population becoming more and more there needs more and more people to do various jobs. To fulfill the needs the caste system could have been originated. After that only caste system became stronger and stronger. This may be due to increase in population. People were conflict to do some jobs. Because of this society could have been in unrest. So Emperors and kings could have divided the people and suppressed them to do some particular jobs. This could have resulted into caste system. This would have grown in bigger way and traditionally followed thousands of year. People lived with ignorance, illiteracy, and poverty. Filling up their stomach was the main reason, beyond that they cannot do any things. Always there were wars among the kings that resulted people not to thinks anything else. People lively wood was at the stake. The caste system could have helped the kings to rule state peacefully and without major problem.

So the caste system was at its peak. One caste people cannot walk on the other caste people street. Those who are doing poojas to God and nearby God that is temple are believed to be the higher castes. And those who are all helping to them and providing material to God worship is considered next to them. Like that stage by stage caste system could have been grown. It continued like that thousands and thousands of years. People are respecting the higher caste as it was tradition feeling and practice.

This feeling has grown thousands and thousands of years ago. Exploitation was done within the name of caste also. Some people will do work and some people get profit. This exploitation was there even inside the same caste between have and have not's. Rich people will not take marriage alliance from poor people even in the same caste. This is the pride and prestige. In such case how they allow mixing of the other caste.

After independence there is a lot of change in India. Government is taking all steps to eradicate the inequality and casteism. But it will not die so soon and will take some more time for completion. Now all the castes are fighting for the reservation in jobs, education and so on. If the same trends continuous castes definitely will exist.

Nowadays even though castes exist, caste feeling is not there in urban areas; almost they accept love or inter caste marriages.

All section of the people are living in the same status and equally earning. The children are much matured and moving with each other not bothered about caste or creed even though there is economic difference. They help for each other and fight for their friends. But in the village side still they are not able to come out the traditional feeling. Their ego and minds are not accepting the equality status.

They much attached to the caste and community system. Old people have very much caste feeling because they have not participated people and society growth.

This is due to illiteracy, not able to come out of their traditional customs, not understanding the feeling of others, lack of awareness of the world scenario and value of life. This will definitely change within another two generation. When it will change is the question? Some caste will feel that they are not able to mix and marry in higher caste but not agree to mix and marry below their castes. Actually there is no lower and higher caste, but it was created by the society to carry out the regular jobs. It is like an office job where peon to general manger exists. How human beings can be created or born from different origin? The varnas concept is very much false.

It makes fool of the human origin. If you feel that your higher caste, the lower caste person is nothing but your brother only. People forget to feel that where the lower caste is comes. Urban and city people understands that castes system is created by the olden society and no value, but village people still believe the castes system, it is due to their inborn hundreds years of practice and feel that they higher caste that somebody. Even educated people in village side have caste feeling. They do not have heart to accept lower caste person as an officer in any organization.

They tolerate only because of government rules and regulation. They do not think that how the lower caste would have come? All the human being is brothers and sisters only. Only somebody feel very happy that they are higher caste than somebody else. When they are rejected by the higher caste they feel but not rectify their mistake. But actually nobody wants to follow caste system nowadays, but only caste village system restricts the people. Boys and girls in villages are studying well and mingle with each other without caste and religious feeling. They help each other and find jobs like city students. But village parents are not coming forward to accept their children feeling because of their society caste bondage. Political parties are also helping for this to get votes. Especially ladies have very much caste feeling. Ladies organization is not doing to eradicate castes feeling among ladies society so far.

They fight for ladies freedom and equality but not the awareness of castes system. No politician coming forward to eradicate caste system but fight for the caste reservation. If his system continuous, it is not possible to eradicate caste system even after thousands of years. It is possible only if all the schools not registering students caste and religion.

Students can practice their religion and other thing in their home not in the school. Government can take care to uplift economically backward people that will cover all section of the people. But party democratic system will not come forward to implement this system; it is possible only by the new democratic system. The new democratic candidate will have disinterested feelings.

31
PARTY THREATS

Party threats are common in India. Party workers interfere in all the matters. Ruling party introduces any benefit to public or poor people that benefit distributions are handled by ruling party office bearers only. Majority benefited people will be those who are related to ruling party or supporter of the ruling party. Opposite ruling parties, other parties make use of this opportunity and make agitation, violence and unrest. If the opposition party comes to power they will also doing the same mistake. With the support of the party their follower dare enough to do any violence, criminal work and good work also.

Law and order will be mostly in support of parties only. Getting any genuine thing also we require some party support. People, police and judges are not spared by political parties. Suddenly parties can organize anything; they have lot of money power and man power.

If one national party leader says something or undergo any reference that party followers make the whole nation to burn and keep the nation in turmoil.

In the present period no single party is winning two third majorities, coalition government is the only way to form the government; in future it will be more pathetic. Now at least two or three parties only needed to support, in future more parties need to support the government, due to growth of the so many regional parties.

Sometime supporting parties are not supporting the good plans and programmes of major single party government. So that good plans and programme also will be dropped. Sometime supporting parties will put forth some demand which the major party has to fulfill by closing their eyes. Major single party also very ambitious, they want to rule the nation by some other means, they want to be always in power.

If the **new democratic system** is introduced these problems will not be there since all the elected MPS and MLAs are part of the government. Any bill can be passed by two third majority of the parliament or assembly, otherwise it will be dropped.

There no opposition candidates to question the bill passed by the parliament or assembly since majority of the elected candidates supported the bill.

Any new plan, price fixation, taxation will take place smoothly. Elected member will be doing for the benefit of the nation only. They will not be doing unnecessary taxation, subsidies and free thing in order to get votes.

32
CORRUPTION

"Corruption an easy and intellectual way of earning"

Corruption is a worldwide disease. India ranks in topper ten lists. Thanks to Indian democracy and Indian people attitude and culture.

In India everywhere there is corruption, all departments are corrupt, corruption becoming a common practice in India. Nobody feels shy on this; because people in the high position are more corrupt than down the line people. Common people, working class people, labors cannot earn money in the illegal way. Rich people employ them as bonded labor and pay them meager wages, but pay for somebody lump sum to cover up.

Why this corruption practice is continuing? What may be the reasons? Where it could have been started?

This should be analyzed deeply. First it could have been started in the Kings olden period. Kings has to pay lump sum (Kappam) to Emperors, Jamins has to pay Lump sum to the kings. Common people have to pay jamins or village head for getting something even getting genuine things.

Later on it has been transformed into corruption to do some favor. This is practiced first in higher level. When democracy came to power, the power was distributed to ministry and government offices. Since political parties are ruling the country and politicians are having the influence to do so many things. So Politicians have lot of powers and influences and know the loop holes so they can solve any problems easily. Going by legal way the problem may not be solved so easily so people approaches politicians and pay to them and achieve what they want.

State and central government official and staff have also a lot of power to use or misuse. They can delay any work saying so many reason at the same time they do the same work in fast manner by applying short cut ways. They can twist the normal thing into complicated manner. Who can enquire and find out the truth? Why this is happening means that all wants easy money and wants to live good wealth in the society.

Want to mint money in short time for their family and children. They do not believe their children that they will earn their own livelihood. By minting money they want to keep their entire hereditary in good wealth.

Politician may have only short time in power and at any time he can be thrown out so that he wants to make use of it. If a minister serves one term he can earn wealth for ten hereditary the saying goes. Then how much will be if a person who is always minister. Which political leader talks about corruption in general in the meetings? They talks about other parties' corruption. Other party made so much loss to the government; earned so much money not about their own party and their own people.

So there is a need to stop this practice and remove this disease from the society. We need a clean society. Everybody has to work and earn and live with dignity and pride. Doing any work is not same, whether cleaning the sewage, sweeping the toilet, sweeping the street, doing agricultural work and so on. We should fill our stomach by the hard earned money not with any money. Do not think too much about our future, family and children and do the corruption. Think off that they can live happily without your corrupt money and lead a perfect, clear and good way of life. How it can happen? When it can happen?

In the present democracy system alternatively people can come to the power and nullify their mistakes. There are a lot of lope holes to come to the power. People have no choice but they have to elect the same people. So they are doing mistake without any fear.

In the new democratic system he is not confident of coming to power again so he will not do much harm to the society. People have choice to elect candidate of their own choice. If it is straitened automatically the entire government department will get straitened and get more or less clean society. Everybody has to work and earn money for their living. Why should we accumulate money cheating others or cheating government?

These thinking have to come in everybody mind. Why poverty is growing because the money is accumulate in the pockets of 20 to 30 % of the people. 50% are common employees meeting their day to day needs. Others are labors and poor people. So the new democracy is the only solution to remove the corruption in society. It is possible only in **new democracy**, not in the present political party system.

33

TERRORISM

"Terrorism is outburst of feeling of some section of affected people"

"Root causes are nothing but the Governments, religions; region and nations"

Why terrorism in the world, what is the major reason for the growth of the terrorism in the world?

One has to think deeply to its root causes. One reason is that the suppression of one section of the people by other section. Another reason is ambitious people wants to dominate others to enjoy the life. Another strong reason is religious feeling. Finally it is the Government negligence in not taking enough care on those who are always suppressed. Even democratic country like India is celebrating the Independence Day by having lakhs of security personnel.

President and Prime minister have to address the gathering in bulletproof cabins. Ministers and VIPs have to travel with full security and safety. The expense incurring is huge. How to eliminate the terrorism?

The main reason for terrorism is suppression, government negligence, blind religion feeling, religious intolerance, inferiority complex and involvement of political and religious leaders.

First of all international level political leaders should not suppress any country by their money and muscle power. At national level there should not be any religious party.

All section of the people should be involved or engaged in some kind of work. Peoples' minimum need should be met to divert from involving the illegal activities and go in the wrong way.

Often political leader should address the public the importance of life and peace rather than preaching their policies and their party achievements. Rich people should not contribute money and materials to terrorism by way of religious sentiments. Countries should not supply arms and ammunitions to the terrorist. One country should not suppress other country in any way of dealing.

If the new democratic system comes into force, all section of the people will get their minimum requirement by the help of their elected leaders. So there won't be any crisis for agitation. Now the elected leaders rarely visit the constituency. They will not enquire what their needs and properly listens their demands, because they cannot solve their problem, only their party high command can decide.

Party high command will think in country level, not interested in small scale level.

Due this negligence, the affected people want to fulfill their demands by some other means. If they fight in legal way they will be harassed and put into jail, and fix them in so many false cases.

Government, political parties and police and judiciary all are very expert in doing all this kind. Those who go in support of them also will undergo the condition, so no one will come forward. The net result is taking the arms into their hands whatever may happen whether there is success or failure. Ego is major factor both the sides not coming for negotiation.

In the new democratic system it is simple. The local man only will contest in election, he know what are the demands of that area. So local people will elect the proper MLAs or MPs. He can very well put forth all the demands in parliament or in assembly and get the problem solved. He can very well convince their people and tell them whether it is possible or not and how much time it will take to meet their demands. In present party system nobody is in a position to give clear picture.

34

STRIKES

"Strikes are out burst of Tolerance"

Working class use to do strike to get salary increase, bonus and perks. Labors do strike for their wage increase and for other benefits. Government will negotiate with the striking people and solve the problem. If they are not agreed government will deal with iron hand and disperse the people by so many ways of treats even though their demand is genuine.

If people feel that government is not taking any correct measures for their demands then they will get disappointed. So the affected people, agitated masses and dissatisfied classes only way is to go on strike to achieve their goals. To express the feeling in mass way is the only solution rather than individual fighting. Government or any management is listening the causes if only masses express the demands, otherwise nobody listens the demands even if it is genuine. Nowadays public doing strike and agitation for their demands like improving infrastructure, water facilities, roads and transport etc. Political parties are doing baundh hunger strike and agitation to show their dissatisfaction on ruling government wrong policy and attitudes, for the interest of people, religion, and language and so on. The possibility of the baundh and agitation in New Democracy may be Minimum.

35

PRICE CONTROL

Purely the policy of the government is the main reason for the price fluctuation. Ruling party always thinks and concentrates on its growth and on its power continuation. So they want to favor some section of the people, which may result to achieve their goals.

Change in government in states and central causes enormous loss in our country. New government sometimes throw the plan and policy of the previous government just like that and start their own policy and programme which may result enormous loss to the country. Government always favor the rich people to get their party fund to use for the election expenses and favor lower class masses to get their solid votes. The middle class and upper middle class people most tax payers will not be mostly considered for anything. These people no other goes pay all the taxes, under go all the suffering, even after suffering they will madly support some party and work for that party benefit. All parties aware of this situation, so increase in price will not give much effect for the ruling party. In new democratic system there will not be any change in the programme, policy from the earlier government to new government.

The new government has to follow the previous government policy and programme so that government money not evens a single paisa will be in waste. There is no option for the new government to blame the previous government. This is not based on party politics. Now one party is blaming other party for the failures. This will not happen in the new system of democracy.

The elected MLAs and MPs are individuals; all the elected members are the part of the government.

They have to do all the best things for the country and people. Each election there will be change in person holding the portfolio and ministry. In such situation there will be solid growth and development will take place in the country.

36
POVERTY

"Poverty is only for human beings, but one can come out of it by hard work"

As of now India is having more than 20% of total population are under poverty line. If your income is Rs 360/- per month you are not under poverty line some saying goes.

Indians are very best in interpretation. They can interpret same thing in favor if they want and speak against if they do not want. Indians are very best in believing all things.

This is Indian democracy. Even after 70 years of independence why the poverty is not controlled. It is increasing only. Are any defects in our policy? Are it is maintained purposefully? In food production India is self-sufficient; then why people are suffering for food? India got vast land then why people are suffering for shelter? India is exporting cotton then why people are suffering for cloths? Why so many beggars are in the street?

Any development happens it is only after people request and agitation. Ruling government will concentrate on only profit making.

Economically weaker sections people are only going to the Government hospital, but there is no sufficient doctors, nurses and attenders. Beyond that there is no medicine. Most of the equipment is not in working condition.

What will be the fate of the common people health? All good and experienced doctors are employed in Government hospitals only, but they cannot use their full capacity since the not availability of the men and materials.

Village health centers not properly supported and maintained. Doctors are not interested to work in villages, since they cannot get city atmosphere and earning.

Sometimes poor people also go to private hospital to save their health by borrowing or selling their property and belongings. But private hospitals charges differ from hospital to hospital. There is no control on tests and charges. They try for maximum income.

To eradicate the poverty, area wise survey has to be taken and proper long term plan and implementation needed.

37

ELIGIBILITY CRITERIA

MLAs & MPs candidates' eligibility criteria to contest in the election.

Candidates should be born in that constituency or native of that constituency or permanent residence of that constituency and should have completed 25 years of age and below 70 years. Candidate should have minimum graduate degree from recognized Indian university. (inclusive of engineering degree, doctors degree and law degree etc.) Mentally and physically sound and free from criminal case. Candidate shall not mention his/her caste and religion in the examination form. Name, father or mother name, native place and date of birth and gender and its proof are enough. Candidate should write examination conduct by respective election commission and come within 15th rank.

Candidate can write only three times to qualify. All the fifteen candidates can contest in the election. Candidates already wrote the examination and won in election can contest directly at any number of time.

But if they lose in three elections they are not eligible to contest in election. Candidates should write separate examination for MLAs and MPs. After election who score highest vote will be MLA or MP. The second rank candidate will get 50% of salary and perks of MLA or MP. The third ranked candidate will get 30 % of salary and perks of MLA or MP. The other 12 candidates will get 20% of salary and perks of MLA or MP for five years till next election. The salary and perks are applicable for other post also like mayor, councilor, panjayat president and ward members.

Member of Parliament

Candidates should be an Indian born, above 25 years and below 70 years, should be minimum a graduate and should be within 15 rank in the examination conducting by election commission for MPs selection. He/she should be native of that Constituency. Mentally and physically sound and free from criminal case. Candidate shall not mention his/her caste and religion in the nomination form. A candidate can write examination for three times only and should come within 15 rank for contesting in election. If a candidate won in any election he can directly contest in election along with 15 candidates.

Candidate passport size photo and name is the symbol for contesting in election.

Member of Legislative Assembly

Candidates should be an Indian born, above 25 years and below 70 years, should be a graduate and should be within 15 ranks in the examination conducting by election commission for MLAs selection. He/she should be native of that Constituency. Mentally and physically sound and free from criminal case. Candidate shall not mention his/her caste and religion in the nomination form.A candidate can write examination for three times only and should come within 15 rank for contesting in election. If a candidate won in any election he can directly contest in election along with 15 candidates. Candidate passport size photo and name is the symbol for conducting in election.

Other Posts

A degree holder is eligible for Mayor and councilors and they should come within 10th positions in the examination conducted by election commission. A 12th passed candidate is eligible for chairman and village president and 10th passed for ward member they should come within 10th positions in the examination conducted by election commission and should be native of that place, above 25 years, mentally and physically sound and free from any criminal cases. All the candidates who come under 10th position are eligible to contest in any election but three times if they lose not eligible for further election. Candidate passport size photo and name is the symbol for conducting in election.

Candidate shall not mention his/her caste and religion in the nomination form.

President of India

Candidate shall be Indian born, below 70 years, should have served at least one full term as a cabinet minister or served as Vice president. Mentally and physically sound and free from criminal case. A person can serve as president for two terms only.

Vice President

Candidate shall be Indian born, below 70 years, should have served one full term as a cabinet minister. Mentally and physically sound and free from criminal case. A person can serve as vice president for two terms only.

Prime Minister

Candidate shall be Indian born, below 70 years, should have served two full terms as a cabinet minister or served full term as Deputy Prime Minister. Mentally and physically sound and free from criminal case. A Person can be served as Prime Minister for two terms only.

Deputy Prime Minister

Candidate shall be Indian born, below70 years, should have served one full term as a cabinet minister. Mentally and physically sound and free from criminal case. A Person can be served as Deputy Prime Minister for two terms only.

Lok sabha Speaker

Candidate should be an Indian born, below70 years, should have served one full term as a cabinet minister. Mentally and physically sound and free from criminal case. A Person can be served as Lok Sabha speaker for two terms only.

Cabinet Minister

He should be an Indian born, below 70 years, should have served one full term as a minister. Mentally and physically sound and free from criminal case. A person can serve as cabinet minister any number of times no restriction.

Union Minister for States

He should be an Indian born, below 70 years, should have served one full term as MP. Mentally and physically sound and free from criminal case. A person can serve has union minister for states any number of times no restriction.

38
ELECTION

Lok Sabha Speaker Election

Present Lok sabha speaker will conduct the election and inform the new speaker name in the Lok sabha. All the newly elected MPs have to assemble in the parliament by 10.00 AM sharp for electing the new Lok sabha speaker. Present Lok sabha speaker will announce in the parliament to file nomination for the Lok sabha speaker position. Half an hour time will be given to file nomination. Interested MPs who served as one term cabinet minister have to file nomination within half an hour through the electronic media provided for them. After that present Lok sabha speaker will announce the eligible candidate's names with passport size photo in the electronic board. Present Lok sabha speaker also can contest in the election and vote for the election if he is eligible. After the instruction all the MPs present in the parliament should vote electronically through the instrument provided for them in their tables.

MPs should not consult each other and speak to each other and not move out of their seats till the results are announced. The candidate who scores the highest votes will be declared as the New Lok sabha speaker. This will be telecasted lively to the public.

President Election

Present president will chair the new president election. Lok sabha Speaker will conduct the election and inform the new President name in the Lok sabha.

All the newly elected MPs have to assemble in the parliament by 10.00 am sharp for electing the new President. Lok sabha Speaker will announce in the parliament to file nomination for the President.

Half an hour time will be given to file nomination. Interested MPs who qualified for the post have to file nomination within half an hour through the electronic media provided for them. After that Lok sabha Speaker will announce the eligible candidate's names with passport size photo in the electronic board. Present President also can contest in the election and vote for the election if he is eligible. After the instruction all the MPs present in the parliament should vote electronically through the instrument provided for them in their tables.

MPs should not consult each other and speak to each other and not move out of their seats till the results are announced. The candidate who scores the highest votes will be declared as the new President the second ranked candidate will be the vice president. This will be telecasted lively to the public.

Prime Minister Election

Present Prime Minister will chair the election of the New Prime Minister. Lok sabha Speaker will conduct the election and inform the new Prime Minister name in the Lok sabha.

All the newly elected MPs have to assemble in the parliament by 10.00 am sharp for electing the new Prime Minister. Lok sabha Speaker will announce in the parliament to file nomination for the Prime Minister. Half an hour time will be given to file nomination. Interested MPs who qualified for the post have to file their nomination for the Prime Minister Position. After that Lok sabha Speaker will announce the eligible candidate's names with the passport size photo in the electronic board. Present Prime Minister also can contest in the election and vote for the election if he is eligible.

After the instruction all the MPs present in the parliament should vote electronically through the instrument provided for them in their tables. MPs should not consult each other and speak to each other and not move out of their seats till the results are announced. The candidate who scores the highest votes will be declared as the New Prime Minister and second ranked candidate will be the deputy Prime Minster. This will be telecasted lively to the public.

Cabinet Minister Election in the Parliament

Parliament will have two type ministers only. One is cabinet minister and another is state minister. Each state will have one minister. There will be only Lok sabha no Rajya sabha.

First of all, Parliament has to decide how many cabinet ministers and other Ministers of state they require to form the government.

Cabinet Minister Election

Lok sabha Speaker will announce the no of cabinet ministers and their portfolios in the Lok sabha. Two days will be given for MPs for their decision. Lok sabha Speaker will conduct the election and inform the newly elected cabinet ministers in the parliament. All the newly elected MPs have to assemble in the parliament by 10.00 am sharp for electing the new Cabinet Ministers. Lok sabha Speaker will announce in the parliament to file nomination for all the Cabinet Ministers position. Half an hour time will be given to file nomination. Qualified MPs have to file their nomination. After that Lok sabha Speaker will announce the eligible candidate's names with passport size photo in the electronic board. Present cabinet Ministers also can contest in the election and vote for the election if he is eligible.

After the instruction all the MPs present in the parliament should vote electronically through the instrument provided for them in their tables.

MPs should not consult each other and speak to each other and not move out of their seats till the results are announced. The candidate who scores the highest votes will be declared as the ministers for the respective position contested. This will be telecasted lively to the public.

Minister of States Election

In the new democratic system there will a minister for each states. Respective sates MPs has to select one Minister to represents their state grievances' directly in the parliament. State MPs have to nominate one electoral officer and conduct the election and elect their respective State Minister.

39

ELIGIBILITY CRITERIA FOR ASSEMBLY ELECTION

Assembly Speaker

He should be an Indian born, below 70 years, should have served one full term as a minister. Mentally and physically sound and free from criminal case. Two terms is the tenure.

Assembly Speaker Election

Present assembly speaker will conduct the election and inform the new assembly speaker name in the Assembly. All the newly elected MLAs have to assemble in the assembly by 10.00 AM sharp for electing the new assembly speaker. Present assembly speaker will announce in the assembly to file nomination for the assembly speaker position. Half an hour time will be given to file nomination.

Qualified and interested MLAs have to file nomination within half an hour through the electronic media provided for them. After that present assembly speaker will announce the eligible candidate's names with passport size photo in the electronic board. Present assembly speaker also can contest in the election and vote for the election if he is eligible. After the instruction all the MLAs present in the assembly should vote electronically through the instrument provided for them in their tables.

MLAs should not consult each other and speak to each other and not move out of their seats till the results are announced. The candidate who scores the highest votes will be declared as the new assembly speaker. This will be telecasted lively to the public.

Chief Minister Eligibility Criteria

He should be an Indian born, below 70 years, should have served two full terms as cabinet minister. Deputy Chief Minister is also eligible for Chief Minister Election.

Mentally and physically sound and free from criminal case. Chief Minister Tenure is two terms only.

Chief Minister Election

Present Chief Minister will chair the New Chief Minister Election. peaker of the assembly will conduct the election and inform the new Chief Minister name in the Assembly. All the newly elected MLAs have to assemble in the assembly by 10.00 AM sharp for electing the new Chief Minister. Speaker of the assembly will announce in the assembly to file nomination for the Chief Minister position. Half an hour time will be given to file nomination.

Qualified and interested MLAs have to file their nomination within half an hour through the electronic media provided for them. After that the speaker of the assembly will announce the eligible candidate's names with passport size photo in the electronic board.

Present Chief Minister also can contest in the election and vote for the election if he is eligible. After the instruction all the MLAs present in the assembly should vote electronically through the instrument provided for them in their tables.

MLAs should not consult each other and speak to each other and not move out of their seats till the results are announced. The candidate who scores the highest votes will be declared as the new Chief Minister and the second ranked candidate will be deputy chief minister. This will be telecasted lively to the public.

Assembly Cabinet Minister Election

Assembly Speaker will announce the no of cabinet ministers and their portfolios in the assembly. Two days will be given for MLAs for their decision. Speaker will conduct the election and inform the newly elected cabinet ministers in the Assembly.

All the newly elected MLAs have to assemble in the assembly by 10.00 am sharp for electing the new Cabinet Ministers. Speaker will announce in the assembly to file nomination for all the Cabinet Ministers position. Half an hour time will be given to file nomination. Qualified MPs have to file their nomination. After that Lok sabha Speaker will announce the eligible candidate's names with passport size photo in the electronic board.

Present cabinet Ministers also can contest in the election and vote for the election if he is eligible. After the instruction all the MLAs present in the assembly should vote electronically through the instrument provided for them in their tables. MLAs should not consult each other and speak to each other and not move out of their seats till the results are announced. The candidate who scores the highest votes will be declared as the ministers for the respective position contested. This will be telecasted lively to the public.

District Minister Election

In the new democratic system there will have one minister for each District. Respective District MLAs has to select one district Minister to represents their District grievances' directly in the Assembly. District MLAs have to nominate one electoral officer and conduct the election and elect their respective District Minister.

40

ELECTION COMMISSION EXAMINATION

Election commission will conduct MLAs & MPs candidate selection examination in the respective areas.

MPs examination will be conducted in each state at same day. MLAs examination also will be conducted at each district at same day. Both the examination will be in different dates. So that candidate can write both the examination. Result will be declared in short duration. All those who score upto 15th rank will be eligible to contest in election. There will be number of people to contest in election. This is the system to filter candidate numbers.

41

THE ABOVE ELIGIBILITY CRITERIA

The above eligible criteria are not possible for the first two general elections. For the first election MPs who are 50 and above are eligible to contest for President, Prime Minister, Lok Saba speaker, cabinet Minister and Ministers. MLAs who are 50 and above are eligible to contest for Chief Minister, Assembly Speaker, Sate Cabinet Minister and District Ministers. For second election some eligible criteria can be relaxed. If the above eligible criteria are not satisfactory, the elected MPs and MLAs can decide and arrive some common eligible criteria.

42

NO CONFIDENCE MOTION

If majority of MPs are not satisfied by the performance of any Minister, President, Vice President and they can table the non-performance activities of that position and that Minister. Table their corruption charges, misuse of power and criminal activities and ask for no confidence motion for their removable. Two third majorities of present MPs have to vote for their removal. Fill up that position MPs should elect a new person as per above method within three months.

If majority of MLAs are not satisfied by the performance of any Minister, Chief Minister, Deputy Chief Minister and they can table the non-performance activities of that position and that Minister. Table their corruption charges, misuse of power and criminal activities and ask for no confidence motion for their removable. Two third majorities of present MLAs have to vote for their removal. Fill up that position MLAs should elect a new person as per above method within three months.

43

RAJYA SABHA AND LEGISLATIVE ASSEMBLY

Rajya Sabha members are President Nominees and Parties Nominees. Since the New Democracy is based on without party system, the nomination will not arise, so there is no need for Rajya Sabha and same to Legislative assembly. Moreover single administration and approval is good for the country development. Person who served as central cabinet Minister can be appointed as governor of state.

44

INDIAN CONSTITUTION

All the functions of the Indian constitution will remain the same, MPs and MLAs electoral process is only chancing in the New Democracy.

45

CONTRIBUTION OF SOCIAL MEDIAS AND NEWSPAPERS AND JOURNALS

All these above fourth column place major role in the country and world. They have to give correct in formation to the society. They should not favor somebody and mislead the society. They should educate the people, to support growth of economy of the country, suppress and remove religious and caste feeling. No doubts that some Medias and newspapers and journals are doing well. But nowadays some are prone to some political parties, regions and religions.

They are moving towards profit orientation never bother about society and country. They became coward of some political power. They give wrong in formation and mislead the society and country. One day they will become unpopular in the country. One cannot cheat others always.

One day it will be exposed. So all these fourth column has to be loyal to all whatever may be situation and see the stability and growth of the country without misleading the society.

46
CONCLUSION

Evolution is continuous process. Revolution is a never ending process. Progress in is life a prospective process. So that we have to readily adapt the changes in life. The new democracy is nothing but evolution, revolution and progress in democracy. It is good for the people, better for the society and best for future. Having not based on any party, leadership and symbol and based on only individual performance there will be major and significant chance over in the system.

The major advantage is that the candidate's contact and characteristic will be known to the public whom they have to select. Public have the opportunity to select and elect good candidates.

The elected representative can perform with freedom; he will not be under anybody pressure, he need not seek anybody permission to do any favor to his constituency.

The elected representative has to perform well and cannot escape from the promises which he commits.

All the elected members are the ruling party; they will have better coordination among themselves and do better government. There is a limited opportunity for the elected representatives to misuse or waste country economy just like that. 70 lacs crores Indian money is in Swiss bank the saying goes and rumors persist. Who are the money holders? Is it from rich income group or Politicians or actors or business man or middlemen or inclusive of all these?

If it is so, where from they got so much money and getting so much money? What are the sources? Is it Indian money? Is it money evaded from tax? Why are they depositing in Swiss bank? Why not in India? Is it India not safe? Is it the wrong policy of the Indian government made them to deposit in Swiss? May be true or may not be true.

Government laying enormous Taxes, everything there is Tax, for all thing government wants many irrelevant statements, so that moneyed people fed up and wants to hide their money may be one reason.

They have confidence on Swiss bank but not with the Indian bank and any other banks. They have gone to the extent that even they lose their money they do not worry.

How and when they will get back that money is also not clear? Is India is not safe for deposit? Is India is lack of any secret policy to hold such money? If India has some valuable secret policy to hold this money, this money can be used for our country development. Indian will speak truth and moral value outside only, but practice nothing inside. How to plug these banking activities? What are the remedial measures to arrest this illegal transaction? Ordinary people cannot deposit in Swiss bank, only big people can do it, it is evident and clear. Party less politics is good for our country at present. There will be less corruption, rare murder and nil law and order problem. In the party less system who is there to organize any activities, where will be the masses to support the unlawful deeds?

Because of the party background so many good things also happening now, we cannot deny that. But because of the party background only corruption is increasing every day in nook and corner of the country. To get even individual basic facilities and infrastructure we have bribe government officials and politicians otherwise work will not be done. Money making is a common and way of passion in somebody life.

If a man does not use the chance and make money he will be considered as useless in the society. Some are less ambitious, some are more ambitious and some are extremely ambitious. But any Party people and politician cannot be charged so easily. Nobody dare to touch them either by law and order or by judiciary.

Even if they are charged they will come out easily. They have money power and mass muscle power. First the people will fight for his or her punishment after sometime the same people will start sympathies for them and support for their release. The same way some opposition parties tactically doing, first they will argue for the punishment, later on they will let lose because the same thing come for his party people also.

So politician will escape somehow or other, only rare politician will get punishment. Rules and regulations are only for common and destitute people. For ruler and law makers for making money the government officials and staff has to help, otherwise they will not be in that post. Sometimes the helpers also will have share, otherwise make some other ways to achieve their special shares. Some extremely ambitious categories will make special way to achieve their goals.

One should think that in new democratic system an individual person cannot make a grave mistake even if comes to top most position in the ruling government. He cannot do beyond certain limit, because he has no outside support, there is no mass chain or mass support for his action.

Since he is not having enough mass support he will be afraid of doing illegal things and there is nobody to argue him to do so. Every five years the parliamentarian will change, their portfolio will change and all in the hands of the elected members. There is no one man show here. Here there is no opposition party to take revenge on earlier rulers, only opposition candidates who will also in favor of the people and developments.

Any project started will be completed and will not drop abruptly whatever may be the change in parliamentarians. So it is high time to have this new democratic system and all people should come forward for its implementation. This kind of independent candidate election will pay a way for the good democracy.

It will create good and powerful leaders and our country will be an ideal country in the world. No political party or leader will come forward to implement this new democracy. Those who are benefited by the party system will not support this democracy change. There will be lot of criticism and negative approach from big people. They will divert the people against this New Democratic system saying that it is useless and not practicable. The implementation is not so easy. It is only on the hands of the people. People with courage, confidence and boldness have to come forward and elect independent candidates.

People should create awareness one among themselves about this New Democratic system. They should educate the advantages and benefits of this system to the society. Then only common people believe and understand this New Democracy.

Each and every one has to strongly take action to blossom the New Democracy. Everybody has to share the democracy and it should not be under one man and one party control. What is the difference between king's rule and party system? It is one and the same. So people should elect independent candidates only in the forthcoming elections. If majority are independent candidates then New Democratic system will automatically come out. Otherwise we have to be slave of the party system and caste, creed, religion and language problem will persist and these problems will never die.

So people have to think, think, think and deeply think and implement this New Democracy. Actually no political party and politicians are not in favor of caste, creed, religion and language but to mobilize votes they have to support for all these factors. It is really people sentiments and weakness. But if all are individual candidates there is no place for these sentiments and weakness. All will be treated equally.

So people have to think deeply and come forward to elect independent candidates in the forth coming election.

Again I assure that no political party and politician will come forward to implement this New Democracy. Because of the party system they are enjoying the power and fame lifelong. They want masses to respect and protect them. By party system they can mobilize funds and do anything.

Only real politician who wants everyone growth and development will come forward to implement this New Democracy. Social organization, Social workers and some welfare organizations have to come forward and create awareness among people to implement this system. But one day the New Democratic system will blossom not only in our country but also throughout the world.

Good luck.

Thank you all.

The Author.

www.ingramcontent.com/pod-product-compliance
Lightning Source LLC
Chambersburg PA
CBHW031126250726
48655CB00002B/539